WHAT IS ART?

Photography

KAREN HOSACK

CHICAGO, ILLINOIS

Editorial: Adam Miller, Charlotte Guillain, Clare Lewis,
and Catherine Veitch
Design: Victoria Bevan and AMR Design Ltd
Illustrations: David Woodroffe
Picture Research: Mica Brancic
and Helen Reilly/Arnos Design Ltd
Production: Victoria Fitzgerald

Originated by Modern Age
Printed and bound by CTPS (China Translation and
Printing Services Ltd)

13 12 11 10 09
10 9 8 7 6 5 4 3 2 1

Library of Congress Cataloging-in-Publication Data
Hosack, Karen.
  Photography / Karen Hosack.
    p. cm. -- (What is art?)
  Includes bibliographical references and index.
  ISBN 978-1-4109-3160-3 (hc)
  1. Photography--Juvenile literature. 2. Composition
(Photography)--Juvenile literature. I. Title.
  TR149.H67 2008
  770--dc22
                                          2008009693

Acknowledgments
The publishers would like to thank the following for
permission to reproduce photographs:
Copyright of the artist, Courtesy Anthony Reynolds
Gallery p. **7**; © Scala, Florence p. **20** (© Man Ray
Trust/ADAGP, Paris and DACS, London 2008); ©The
Bridgeman Art Library pp. **10** (Gemaeldegalerie
Alte Meister, Dresden, Germany/Staatliche
Kunstsammlungen Dresden), **21** (© Salvador Dali,
Gala-Salvador Dali Foundation, DACS, London 2008),
22 (Museo di Storia della Fotografia Fratelli Alinari,
Florence, Alinari), **27** (Private Collection, Archives
Charmet); ©The British Library p. **4**; © Corbis pp.
5 (Ansel Adams Publishing Rights Trust), **12** (The
Andy Warhol Foundation for the Visual Arts), **15** (Joe
Rosenthal); ©David Hockney p. **8**; Digital Image © The
Museum of Modern Art
p. **6** (Licensed by SCALA/Art Resource, NY); with kind
permission from Ellen Ugelstad p. **9**; ©Getty pp. **15b**
(2001 The Record (Bergen Record, N.J.) Photo by
Thomas E. Franklin), **24** (TimeLife pictures/Andreas
Feininger); ©International Center of Photography (ICA)
p. **18**; ©Jeff Wall p. **19** (Tate Gallery, London, Great
Britain); ©Panos Pictures p. **17** (Georg Gerster); ©Rex
Features Ltd pp. **14**, **25**; ©Science Photo Library
pp. **16** (Prof. Harold E. Edgerton), **26** (Adam
HartDavis); ©Sothebys p. **13**; ©Tom Hunter p. **11**
(The Saatchi Gallery); ©Tony Howell p. **23**.

Cover photograph of lemon splashing into water
reproduced with permission of Getty Images/
Photonica/VEER George Diebold.

Every effort has been made to contact copyright
holders of any material reproduced in this book.
Any omissions will be rectified in subsequent
printings if notice is given to the publishers.

Disclaimer
All the Internet addresses (URLs) given in this book
were valid at time of going to press. However, due
to the dynamic nature of the Internet, some addresses
may have changed, or sites may have changed or
ceased to exist since publication. While the author
and publishers regret any inconvenience this may
cause readers, no responsibility for any such changes
can be accepted by either the author or the publishers.
It is recommended that adults supervise children
on the Internet.

Contents

Any words appearing in the text in bold, **like this**,
are explained in the glossary.

Photography and Art

Ever since the first camera was used in 1827, people have used photography to record many things. Some people use cameras to capture personal special events, like birthdays or weddings. **Journalists** take photographs to show moments in history.

Some artists use photography either as a tool to help them produce a final work or as the final work itself. Here, two artists have taken photographs instead of painting a picture. The process of making the image is very different from painting.

"The Haystack" by William Henry Fox Talbot, c. 1844

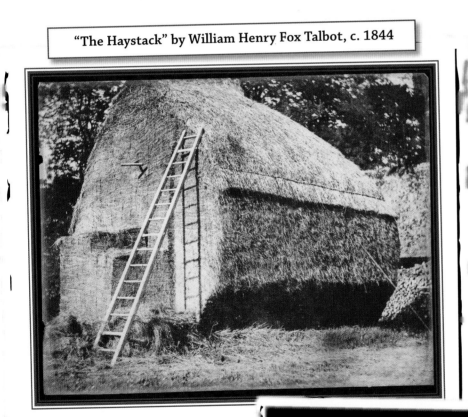

The artist has set up the scene so we think that the people building the haystack have only been gone for a short while. What clues help you to think this?

"Moonrise over Hernandez" by Ansel Adams, 1941

In the early photograph opposite, we can see a haystack on a sunny day. We can tell that it must be summer, because that is when people make hay.

The photograph above of the moon rising also makes us think about how people are involved in a **landscape**. But the photograph does not show anyone. How has the artist done this?

Telling a Story

What can we tell about this woman by just looking at the photograph? The photographer has spent time making sure the image is lit well. The light makes the woman's hat and veil cast a small shadow across her face. This makes her look slightly mysterious. She wears a lot of makeup and jewelry, and we can see she is sitting in a bar.

This woman is not a well-known person, but the photographer has made her look important because of the care he has taken in capturing her character.

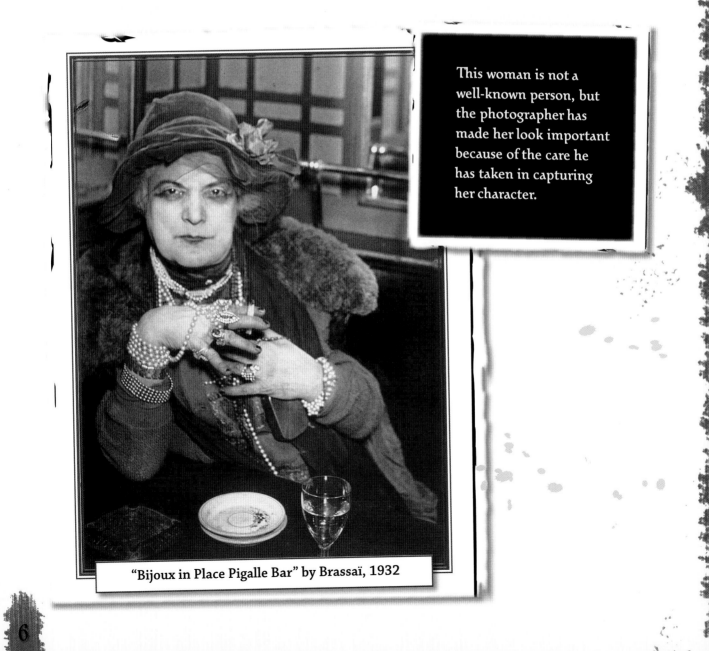

"Bijoux in Place Pigalle Bar" by Brassaï, 1932

The artist who took this photograph only gives us a small amount of information to help us build a story around the character in the image. We have to make up the rest of the story ourselves.

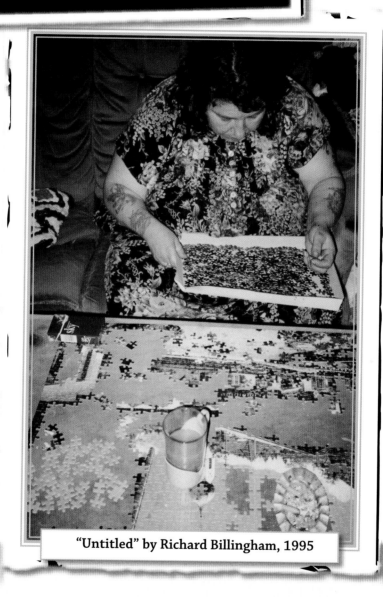

"Untitled" by Richard Billingham, 1995

We do not know about the woman in the photograph above, either. We can see from the image that she enjoys doing jigsaw puzzles. We can make up a story about her life by looking at details in the picture. Her **tattoos** tell us what she might have been like when she was younger. We can see things on the floor and on the old sofa. This makes us think she is fairly poor.

Everyday Lives

The British artist David Hockney took these snapshots of his mother during a day out together. It is a cold rainy day and his mother is wrapped up in a raincoat, sitting outside a ruined graveyard. The artist is trying to tell us several things. First, we can see that his mother is old. By showing her in a graveyard he could be thinking that she will die one day, too. He also took the photographs quickly and put them in a **collage**. The style of the finished image tells us about the mother and son's relaxed and loving relationship.

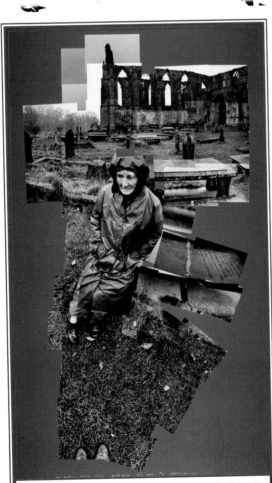

"My Mother, Bolton Abbey, Yorkshire" by David Hockney, 1982

Looking at this photo we get the idea that the artist has a close relationship with his mother.

Polaroid cameras

Before digital cameras were invented, people had to wait for film to be developed before they could see a finished photograph. The Polaroid camera was good for taking quick pictures that were ready in minutes.

"Shoe Project" by Ellen Ugelstad, 2007

The Internet is a great place for sharing photographs. Some artists use it as a way to show their work.

A Norwegian photographer took these pictures of people and their shoes. People have to wear shoes every day for practical reasons. This artist wanted to show that people can show us something about their personality with their shoes. She put the finished photographs on a website.

Photos Inspired by Paintings

This painting is by a Dutch artist named Jan Vermeer. He was very famous for painting scenes of everyday life. These are called **genre paintings**. In this painting we see a young woman reading a letter in front of an open window. Does she look as though she is enjoying what she is reading? Look at her expression. What could be in the letter?

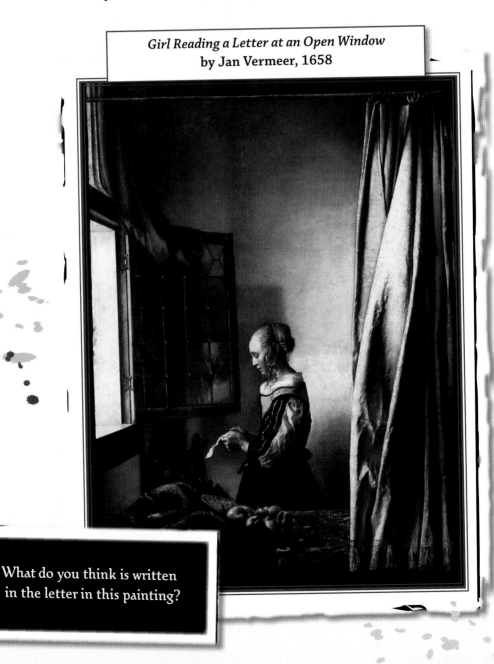

Girl Reading a Letter at an Open Window
by Jan Vermeer, 1658

What do you think is written in the letter in this painting?

Think about it!
This photograph was taken over 300 years after the painting was made. Look at both images carefully and see if you can spot the differences between them. How are they similar?

"Girl Reading a Possession Order" by Tom Hunter, 1998

This photograph is by the artist Tom Hunter. He has set up the same scene, or **composition**, but he has made it in modern-day London. We can see a baby on a bed instead of fruit on the table. The young woman is now dressed in modern clothes and reading a letter in front of a closed window. Does she have the same expression as the Dutch woman in Vermeer's painting?

11

Celebrity

U.S. **Pop artist** Andy Warhol believed that everyone could be famous for 15 minutes. Most of the people he took photographs of were famous for a lot longer. He also made **screen prints** of these celebrities. Warhol would pick a photograph and enlarge it to the size he wanted. He would then transfer it in glue onto the silk screen and roll ink across it. The result was a dramatic image with no wrinkles or lines in the face.

"Marilyn Monroe" by Andy Warhol, 1967 (detail)

Marilyn Monroe was a very famous actress and model in the 1950s and 1960s.

This photograph shows the model Twiggy. She became very famous after her picture was published all over the world.

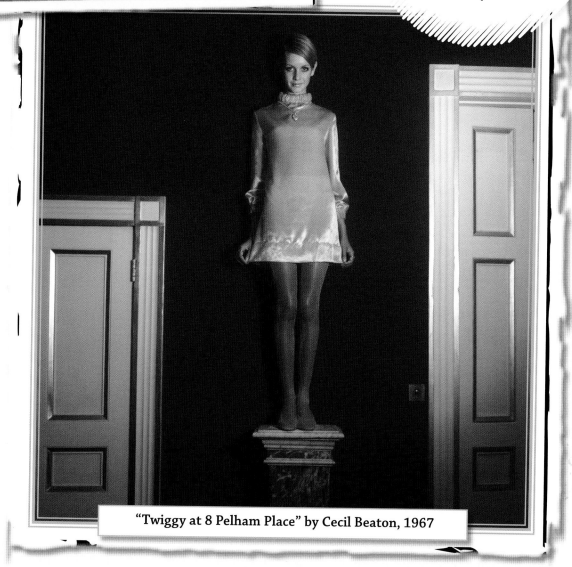

"Twiggy at 8 Pelham Place" by Cecil Beaton, 1967

A fashion photographer took this photograph for a magazine. Fashion photography is supposed to show clothes in a way that will make people want to buy them. Fashion photographs can make people think that buying certain clothes will give them a certain lifestyle. In this photograph the model looks like a beautiful statue.

Powerful Images

This photograph was taken by one of the first people to land on the moon. The moment in history was so important that the photograph has become one of the most famous images of the 20th century. It shows an astronaut named Buzz Aldrin standing on the moon's surface. The photograph also includes the photographer, Neil Armstrong. You can see his reflection in Aldrin's helmet visor. The camera had to be specially designed to work on the moon, where there is no **gravity**. It is an image that shows that humans are capable of incredible things.

Can you spot the astronauts' moon-landing craft, the *Eagle*, reflected in the visor?

"Buzz Aldrin on the Moon" by Neil Armstrong, 1969

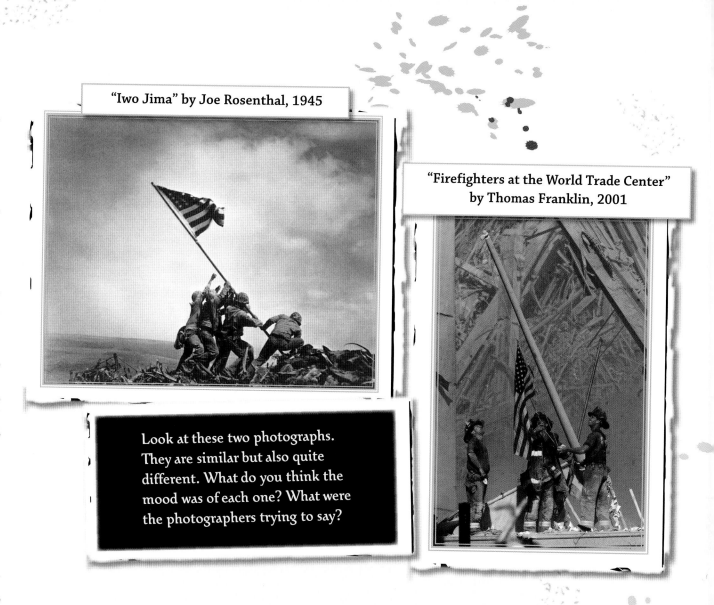

"Iwo Jima" by Joe Rosenthal, 1945

"Firefighters at the World Trade Center" by Thomas Franklin, 2001

Look at these two photographs. They are similar but also quite different. What do you think the mood was of each one? What were the photographers trying to say?

Photographs with powerful messages

Here we see a group of soldiers at the end of World War II, raising the U.S. flag on the Japanese island of Iwo Jima. The United States had just beaten the Japanese. We cannot see the men's faces, so they represent all soldiers. The photograph could also have a more general message about the struggles of war. Another photographer used the same **composition** after the attacks on the United States on September 11, 2001. This time the soldiers were replaced by firefighters.

Things You Cannot Normally See

It would normally be impossible for us to see the shape a drop of milk makes as it falls on a plate. Here the photographer has used a piece of lighting equipment called a **stroboscope**. In the photograph it looks as though time has stopped. The next droplet has already fallen, and another splash is only a second away. The white milk stands out against the red plate, and this helps us see the image as clearly as possible. Harold E. Edgerton also took photographs of bullets shooting in and out of soft materials.

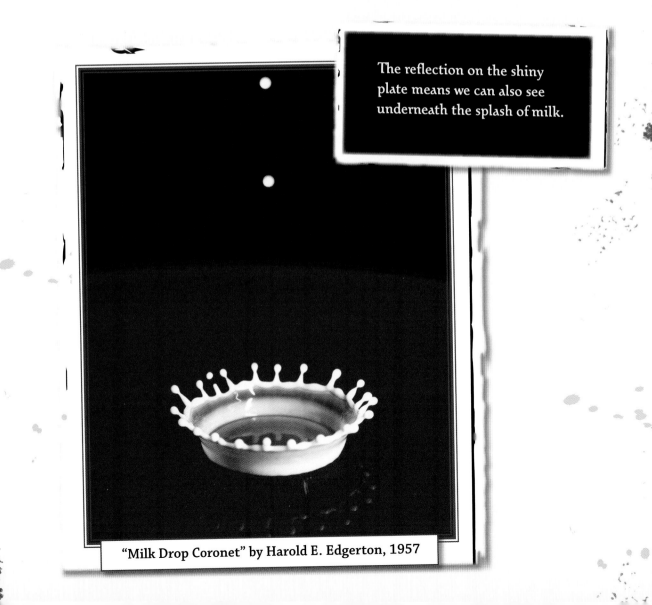

The reflection on the shiny plate means we can also see underneath the splash of milk.

"Milk Drop Coronet" by Harold E. Edgerton, 1957

Do you think the people
who live in this village would
recognize it in the photograph?

Home from the air

It may be possible to see
an aerial photograph of
the place you live on the
Internet on websites such
as Google Earth.

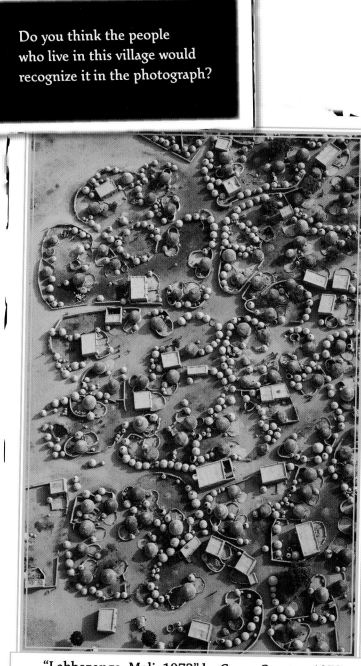

"Labbezanga, Mali, 1972" by Georg Gerster, 1972

Georg Gerster takes many of his photographs from low-flying
planes. This is called **aerial** photography. Here we can see an aerial
shot of an African village. The roofs of the mud huts and the curved
walls between them look like beads strung together on strings. The
overall pattern is not something many people would have seen
before he took the photograph.

Capturing a Moment

This photograph of children on a hot summer's day captures a special moment. When you look at this photograph, you can see how much the children are enjoying themselves. You can almost feel how cold the spray of water is. The children's reactions are clear on their faces as they shout with joy and maybe shock at the cold water. Compare this to the looks on the adults' faces. Do you think they want to join in, too?

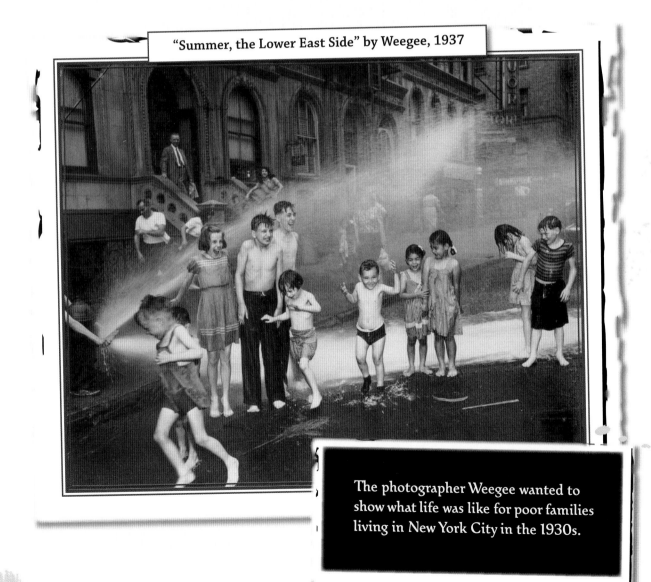

"Summer, the Lower East Side" by Weegee, 1937

The photographer Weegee wanted to show what life was like for poor families living in New York City in the 1930s.

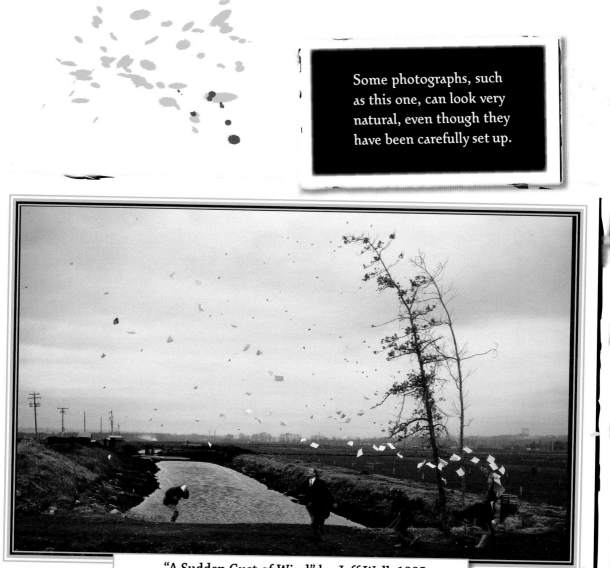

"A Sudden Gust of Wind" by Jeff Wall, 1993

Panic!

This photograph seems to capture a moment, too. We can see people walking in the country by a river. One person is carrying a pile of papers, when a sudden gust of wind lifts the papers from his hands and throws them into the air. The photograph has caught the movements of each person. Two people are trying to stay standing upright in the wind. The man in the center looks as if he wants to help catch the flying papers, but it looks hopeless. In fact, the photographer set up this scene using a group of actors.

Carefully Set-Up Photographs

This photograph was set up by the photographer to look unusual. The tears in this photograph are not real. We can tell this because they are perfectly round and there is no other mark on the model's face. When we cry, tears come out of tear ducts in our eyes. In this photograph there is no sign of where the tears have come from. In fact, these tears are made from glass. Tears are usually a sign of sadness or happiness, but in this photograph the model just stares upward.

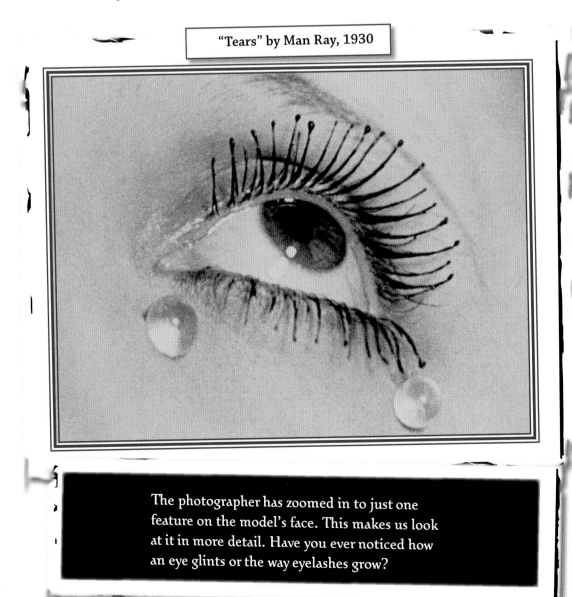

"Tears" by Man Ray, 1930

The photographer has zoomed in to just one feature on the model's face. This makes us look at it in more detail. Have you ever noticed how an eye glints or the way eyelashes grow?

A famous artist named Salvador Dali is in this amazing photograph. oday, an artist could easily use digital technology to create a picture like this. However, this photograph was taken in 1948, before the technology was invented. The photographer had to use assistants who threw the water and cats across the scene as Dali jumped in the air. Other objects were held in the air by thread. The photographer's wife held the chair in position.

"Dali Atomicus" by Philippe Halsman, 1948

Dali

Salvador Dali (1904–1989) was the most famous Surrealist artist. Surrealists tried to realistically paint what might be seen in a dream. Dali's works, although very realistic, contained things you would never see in real life, such as melting clocks.

Philippe Halsman tried to photograph the type of scene that Dali would have painted. Did he succeed?

Altering Images

Look closely at this photograph. Is it a cat or a person? It is actually two photographs. The artist started with a photograph of herself. Then she placed the cat image on top. This is a **negative** on transparent film, so we can see through to the photograph underneath. The final result is a rather creepy **self-portrait** of a "cat woman."

"Cat and I" by Wanda Wulz, 1932

If you were going to make a **portrait** like this of yourself, what animal would you choose for the negative image?

This funny photograph of sheep has been created using more modern technology. The artist has pasted red glowing eyes onto the animals using a computer. It makes the animals look like cartoon characters. Perhaps it also tells us how the artist feels walking through a field of sheep. Does he think they are all watching him?

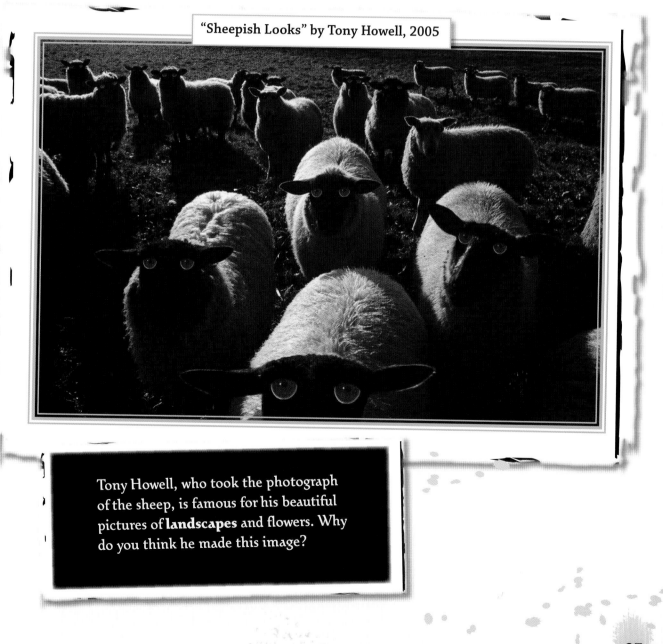

"Sheepish Looks" by Tony Howell, 2005

Tony Howell, who took the photograph of the sheep, is famous for his beautiful pictures of **landscapes** and flowers. Why do you think he made this image?

Photojournalism

When photographs are used to tell the news, it is called photojournalism. Photographers have worked in this way since the 1920s. Andreas Feininger is the photojournalist who took the image below. He used his camera and skills to create a **self-portrait**. He turned the camera on its side so the **lens** and **eyepiece** match the line of his eyes. The top of his camera disguises his nose. It is as though the camera has become part of the photographer.

This picture shows that both the machine and the artist are needed to create photography.

"The Photojournalist" by Andreas Feininger, 1955

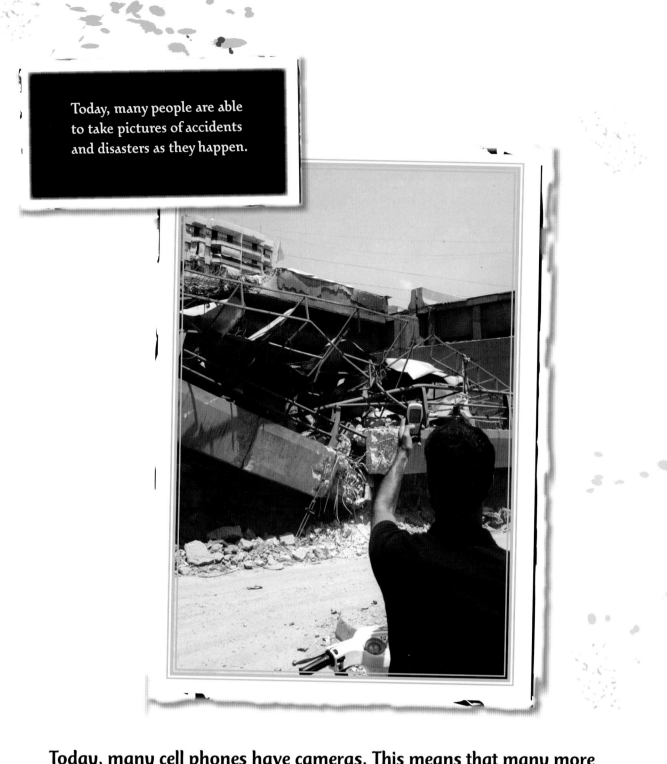

Today, many people are able to take pictures of accidents and disasters as they happen.

Today, many cell phones have cameras. This means that many more people are able to try photojournalism. Television news stations and newspapers ask people to send in photographs and movies of big stories they see around them. Often nonprofessionals are there to take pictures before professional **journalists**. This means that we can now see the most extraordinary photographs of key historical events as they happen.

Moving Pictures

In this book we have looked at the many reasons why people take photographs and how they produce their work. All have been still photographs capturing one moment in time. Today, we are also used to moving images in movies and on television.

One of the first examples of moving images used an instrument called a **zoetrope**. It worked by placing many photographs of a moving subject around the sides of a special wheel.

People would spin the wheel and look at the photographs through small viewing slits. They would see one moving image.

Did you know?

The zoetrope works in a similar way to a flick book. You can make one by drawing a simple picture in the corner of each page of a book. Make each drawing a little different from the last. Flick the pages quickly, and the images seem to move. This is how **animation** used to work.

"Man and Horse Jumping" by Eadweard Muybridge, 1872

As technology changed, it was possible for cameras to capture action as it happened. Twelve cameras were used to take these photographs of a horse jumping. Each camera was started by the last so that the final shots look like they are moving when they are played in order. Even with today's digital technology, this is the basic way that all moving images work.

Timeline

Where to See Photography

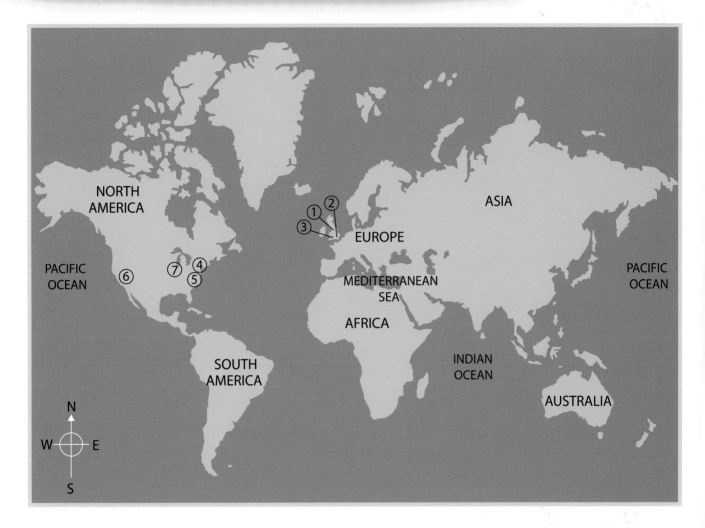

This map shows where some of the best places for viewing photography can be found.

① Bradford, England
National Media
Museum

② London, England
Victoria and
Albert Museum
National Portrait
Gallery

③ Wiltshire, England
Fox Talbot Museum
of Photography

④ New York, New York
The Metropolitan
Museum of Art
International Center
of Photography

⑤ Philadelphia,
Pennsylvania
The Franklin
Institute (history of
photography)

⑥ Los Angeles, California
The Getty Center

⑦ Chicago, Illinois
The Art Institute
of Chicago

Glossary

aerial seen from the air

animation series of pictures shown quickly so they look like a moving image

collage picture made up of lots of smaller pictures

composition how a painting, drawing, or photograph is put together

eyepiece part of a camera that the photographer looks through

frame small picture on a strip of film

genre painting painting showing a scene from everyday life

gravity force that holds us down on Earth

journalist person who reports news events

landscape picture of outdoor scenery

lens curved glass in a camera that focuses light from the subject

negative film that a photograph is first taken with

Pop artist artist belonging to a group of artists who used themes from popular culture in the 1950s and 1960s

portrait painting or photograph of a real person or animal

screen print way of producing the same image many times

self-portrait artist's picture of himself or herself

stroboscope instrument used to make a moving object appear to be stationary

tattoo permanent design made on the skin

zoetrope device that shows many small pictures very quickly so they look like a moving image

Learn More

Books to read

Buckingham, Alan. *Photography (DK Eyewitness Guides)*.
　　New York: Dorling Kindersley, 2004.

Spilsbury, Richard. *Surrealism (Art on the Wall)*. Chicago:
　　Heinemann Library, 2008.

Websites to visit

The website of George Eastman House, a major international
center for studying the history of photography

www.eastmanhouse.org

The International Center of Photography's website

www.icp.org

The website of the National Gallery of Art, which has
a strong photography collection

www.nga.gov/collection/gallery/photo.shtm

Index